LEARNING CHINESE CHARACTER WORKBOOK

学习汉字练习册

The Faster Way to Learn Mandarin Chinese Characters Practice Book

JIA SHENG LOW

CONTENTS

ABOUT THIS BOOK

Learning Chinese should not be a painful experience for you. All the Chinese characters in this workbook were carefully selected to best suit your learning needs. Learning Chinese could be a struggle for beginner learners. This workbook simplifies the whole process of learning Chinese.

Key features of this workbook include:

- ✓ Learners' Guide - this is informative enough for you to learn Chinese. You will learn Chinese strokes, stroke order rules and the Hanyu Pinyin system.
- ✓ Chinese Characters Practice - each Simplified Chinese character is well presented with its radical, stroke count, English definitions and stroke order.
- ✓ This workbook is very suitable for students that plan to take the Hanyu Shuiping Kaoshi (HSK) - a test that is administered by Hanban, an agency of the Ministry of Education of the People's Republic of China.
- ✓ 163 out of 978 new Chinese characters in HSK Level 6 covered.

Are you ready to improve your Chinese language proficiency?

"Tell me and I forget, teach me and I may remember, involve me and I learn." – Benjamin Franklin

LEARNERS' GUIDE

From my experiences of teaching Mandarin Chinese language to both non-native and native learners, in order to master this language, they need to acquire these skills – listen, speak, read, and write. And to acquire these skills, one has to repeat the skill.

While learning those skills isn't as easy as it sounds, it is still not impossible to master it. Apart from the listening, speaking and reading skills, we will focus on writing skills in this book. For many learners of Mandarin Chinese language, one of the most consummate challenges is mastering the Chinese character writing system. Let's dive in!

Chinese Strokes

Chinese characters are written in varying strokes, they are made out of basic strokes. Learning the basic strokes is a must to learning to write Chinese characters.

In modern Simplified Chinese characters, there are over 30 different strokes, with only 8 are the basic ones and all the others are their variants. All strokes have their own name and they have different writing directions.

It is up to you to use pencil, pen or brush to write Chinese characters. As you write Chinese characters, you make dots, lines or hooks one step at a time. The following pages demonstrate 32 Chinese strokes (the first 8 being basic strokes) with explained writing direction. Let's practice it!

Stroke #1	héng (横); Horizontal stroke written from left to right.

Stroke #2	shù (竖); Vertical stroke written from top downward to bottom.

Stroke #3	piě (撇); Left slant stroke written slanting towards the left.

Stroke #4	nà (捺); Right slant stroke written slanting towards the right.

Stroke #5	diǎn (点); The dot is written from top to bottom-right.

Stroke #6	tí (提); Upward stroke from bottom-left to top-right.

Stroke #7	shù gōu (竖钩); Vertical stroke with a hook.

Stroke #8	héng gōu (横钩); Horizontal stroke with a downward hook.

Stroke #9	xié gōu (斜钩); Slant stroke with a upward hook.

Stroke #10	héng zhé (横折); Horizontal stroke with a vertical turn.

Stroke #11	shù zhé (竖折); Vertical stroke with a horizontal turn to the right.

Stroke #12	héng piě (横撇); Horizontal stroke with a down turn to the left.

Stroke #13	piě diǎn (撇点); Downward stroke to the left, and then an extended dot to the right.

Stroke #14	wān gōu (弯钩); Bending stroke with a hook.

Stroke #15	piě zhé (撇折); Down stroke to the left with a turn to the right.

Stroke #16	shù tí (竖提); Vertical stroke followed by a lift to the top right.

Stroke #17	shù wān gōu (竖弯钩); Vertical stroke followed by a level bending stroke with a hook.

Stroke #18	héng zhé gōu (横折钩); Horizontal stroke with downward turn and a hook.

Stroke #19	héng zhé tí (横折提); Horizontal stroke, followed by a vertical one, and then a lift to the top right.

Stroke #20	shù zhé piě (竖折撇); Vertical stroke, horizontal turn to the right, and then a downward turn to the left.

Stroke #21	shù zhé zhé (竖折折); Vertical stroke, horizontal turn to the right, and then a downward vertical stroke.

Stroke #22	héng zhé zhé (横折折); Horizontal stroke, vertical downward turn, and a horizontal turn to the right.

Stroke #23	héng zhé wān (横折弯); Horizontal stroke with a vertical turn and then a bending stroke.

Stroke #24	wò gōu (卧钩); Downward stroke from top left to bottom-right and then a hook.

Stroke #25	héng wān gōu (横弯钩); Horizontal stroke with a turn to the right and an upward hook.

Stroke #26	héng zhé zhé zhé gōu (横折折折钩);Horizontal down to the left,horizontal,down to the left and a hook.

Stroke #27	héng xié wān gōu (横斜弯钩); Horizontal stroke,left slant stroke,horizontal turn to the right and a hook.

Stroke #28	héng zhé wān gōu (横折弯钩); Horizontal stroke, vertical turn, horizontal turn to the right and a hook.

Stroke #29	shù zhé zhé gōu (竖折折钩); Vertical stroke with a double turn and a hook.

Stroke #30	héng zhé zhé piě (横折折撇); Horizontal stroke,downward-left turn,horizontal turn, downward-left turn.

Stroke #31	héng piě wān gōu (横撇弯钩); Horizontal stroke, downward-left turn, downward-right turn and a hook.

Stroke #32	héng zhé zhé zhé (横折折折); Horizontal right, vertical downward, horizontal right, vertical downward.

Stroke Order Rules

Writing Chinese characters according to its rules can remarkably expedite learning in character memorization and recognition. Writing the correct stroke order is important in producing visually enticing characters.

In Mandarin Chinese language, each Chinese character has a standardized stroke order for character formation. In this book, the standardized stroke orders for Simplified Chinese characters are scrupulously based on 《现代汉语通用字笔顺规范》 (Modern Chinese Commonly Used Character Stroke Order Standard) published by 国家语委和中华人民共和国新闻出版署 (China National Language and Character Working Committee and General Administration of Press and Publication of the Peoples' Republic of China) in 1997.

Whether you are right-handed or left-handed, as long as you follow the standardized stroke order rules, you will be able to write appealing Chinese characters. Conventionally, Chinese writing was vertical and went from top to bottom, right to left. Nevertheless, modern Chinese writing uses the western layout of horizontal rows – read from left to right, top to bottom.

To better help you understand how the rules work, the following pages illustrate standardized stroke orders of some chosen Chinese characters. [**Str** (represents Stroke) and **R** (represents Radical) are the abbreviations used in this book.]

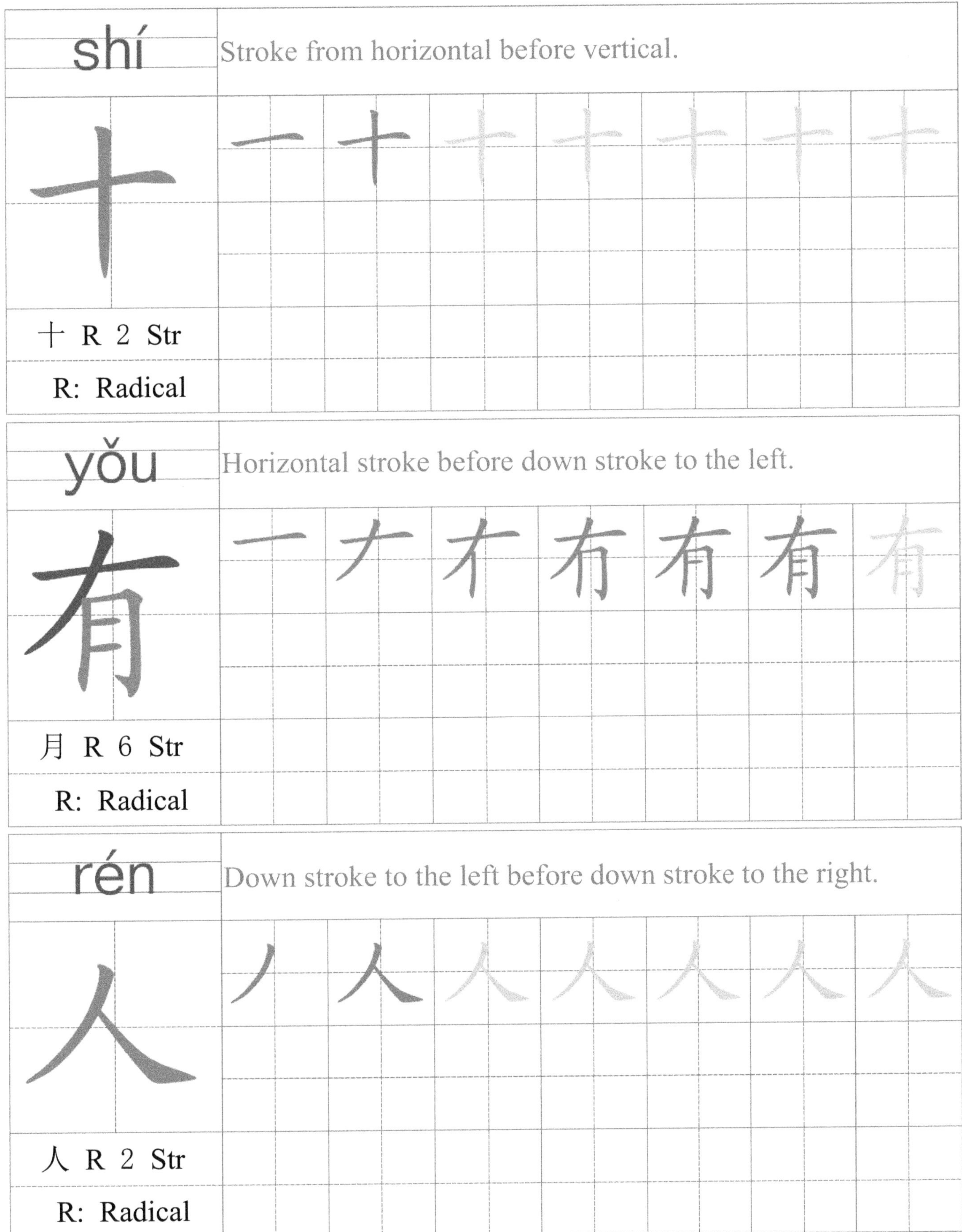
shí
Stroke from horizontal before vertical.
十
一 十
十 R 2 Str
R: Radical
yǒu
Horizontal stroke before down stroke to the left.
有
月 R 6 Str
R: Radical
rén
Down stroke to the left before down stroke to the right.
人
人 R 2 Str
R: Radical

péng	Stroke from down stroke to the left before to the right.
朋	丿 月 月 月 朋 朋 朋 朋 朋 朋 朋 朋 朋 朋
月 R 8 Str	
R: Radical	

sān	Stroke from top to bottom.
三	一 二 三 三 三 三 三
一 R 3 Str	
R: Radical	

rén	Stroke from left to right.
仁	丿 亻 仁 仁 仁 仁 仁
亻 R 4 Str	
R: Radical	

xiǎo	Center verticals before those on both sides.
小	亅 小 小 小 小 小 小
小 R 3 Str	
R: Radical	

yī	Top dot (or upper-left dot, for example, 为) first.
衣	丶 亠 𠂇 衣 衣 衣 衣
衣 R 6 Str	
R: Radical	

fā	Upper-right dot (or inside dot, for example, 瓦) last.
发	𠂉 发 发 发 发 发 发
又 R 5 Str	
R: Radical	

guó
Full Surround Structure: Enclosing strokes first, then inside before bottom enclosing.
国
丨 冂 冃 冃 甪 国 国 国
囗 R 8 Str
R: Radical
sī
Surround from Upper-Right Structure (or Surround from Upper-Left Structure, e.g. 厅): Outside before inside.
司
𠃌 ㇆ 司 司 司
口 R 5 Str
R: Radical
yuǎn
Surround from Lower-Left Structure: Inside before outside.
远
一 二 亍 元 远
辶 R 7 Str
R: Radical

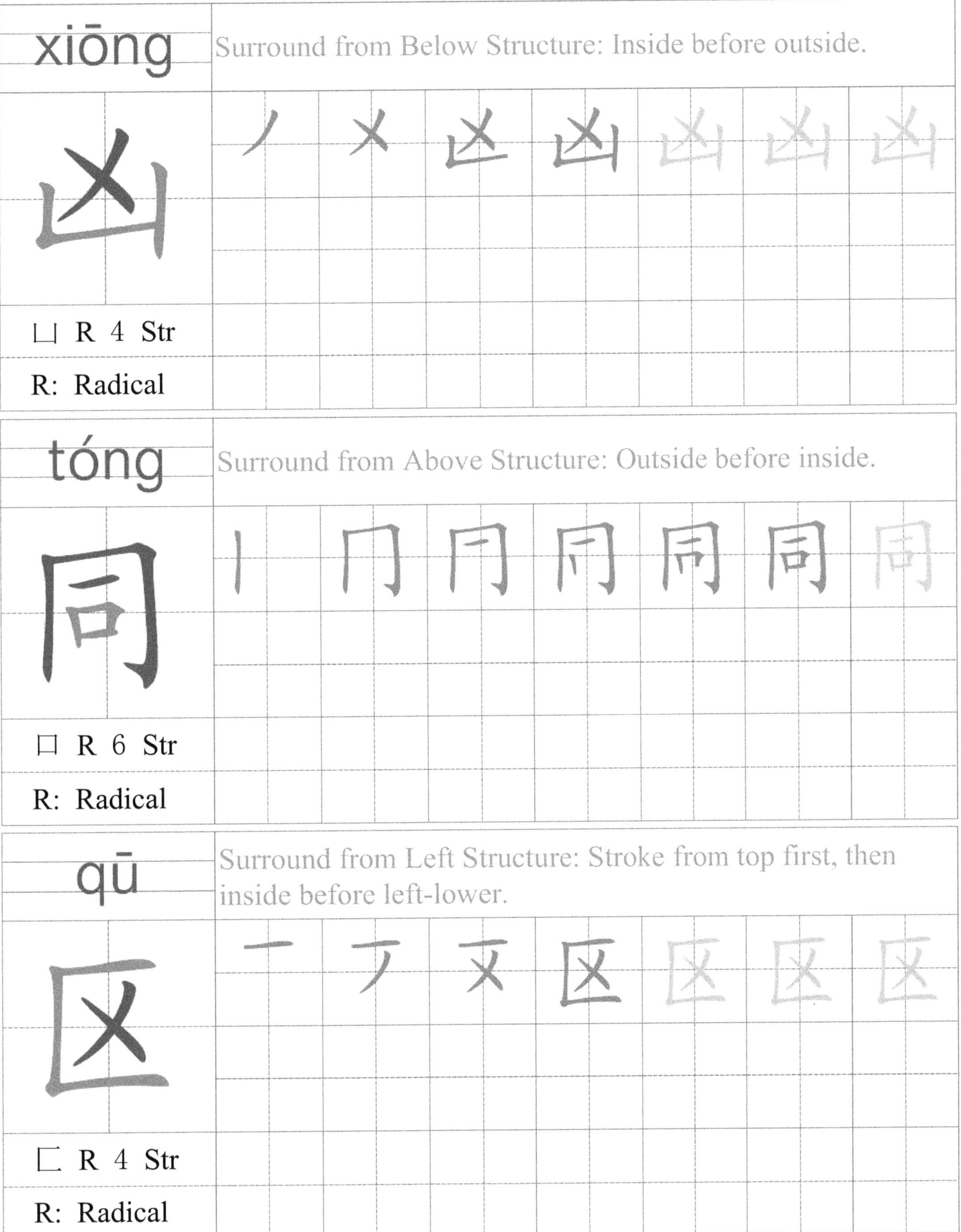
xiōng
Surround from Below Structure: Inside before outside.
凶
凵 R 4 Str
R: Radical
tóng
Surround from Above Structure: Outside before inside.
同
冂 R 6 Str
R: Radical
qū
Surround from Left Structure: Stroke from top first, then inside before left-lower.
区
匚 R 4 Str
R: Radical

The Hanyu Pinyin System

Mandarin Chinese pronunciation used in this book is the Hanyu Pinyin system which is now used almost everywhere in the world. Mandarin Chinese has more than 400 basic syllables, most of them are composed of an initial, a final and a tone mark.

1. Initials

An initial is a consonant that is at the beginning of a syllable. There are a total of 23 initials in Mandarin Chinese language:

b	p	m	f
d	t	n	l
g	k	h	
j	q	x	
zh	ch	sh	r
z	c	s	
y	w		

2. Finals

A final is a vowel that is at the end of a syllable. There are a total of 37 finals in Mandarin Chinese language:

a	an	ang	ai	ao					
o	ou	ong							
e	en	eng	ei						
i	ia	iao	ie	iou (-iu)	ian	in	iang	ing	iong
u	ua	uo	uai	uei (-ui)	uan	uen (-un)	uang	ueng	
ü	üe	üan	ün						
er	ê								

3. Tones

Mandarin Chinese language is a tonal language in which a variation of pitch or tone changes the meaning of the word. There are four tones in Mandarin Chinese language in which each tone is marked by a diacritic. Additionally, there is a neutral tone which is pronounced in a soft and short tone. Hence, it is indicated by the absence of a tone mark. The following page shows a tone chart which illustrates tones using the 5-degree notation. It separates the range of pitches from lowest (1) to the highest (5). Note that the neutral tone is not shown on the chart as it is influenced by the tone that precedes it.

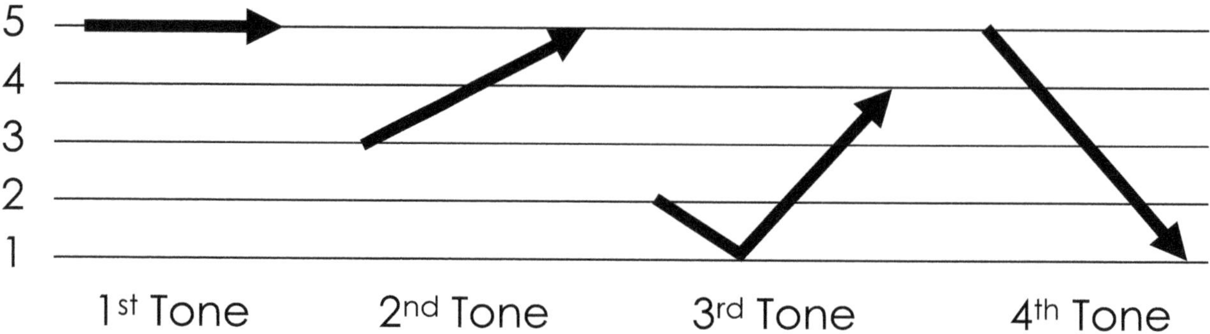

The numbers shown above represent different pitches:

- 5 represents High Pitch.
- 4 represents Medium-High Pitch.
- 3 represents Medium Pitch.
- 2 represents Medium-Low Pitch.
- 1 represents Low Pitch.

Tone	Tone Mark	Explanation
First	ˉ	High and flat tone (55). The pitch starts and remains high.
Second	ˊ	Medium and rising tone (35). The pitch starts at medium-level and rises.
Third	ˇ	Dipping then rising tone (214). The pitch starts at medium-low level, dips to low level and then rises to medium-high level.
Fourth	ˋ	High then falling tone (51). The pitch starts at high-level and falls rapidly to low-level.

4. Tone Marking Rules

Tone marks in Hanyu Pinyin are written directly above the finals. They are marked on the single finals according to this order: a, o, e, i, u, ü.

However, there is a special case for the compound final iu, in which the tone mark is put on the single final u rather than single final i. In this context, many beginner learners may confused it with compound final ui, in which the tone mark is put on the single final i rather than single final u. The rule of thumb is this – whenever single final i and single final u compounded to either compound final iu or compound final ui, the tone mark will be placed on the latter single final, for example, jiù, duī, liú, huī.

When a final beginning with ü combines with j, q or x, the two dots on the top of ü should be omitted, for example, ju, qu, or xu. Nonetheless, if the initial is l (lowercase of alphabet "L") or n, the form is lü and nü sequentially. Examples in this case: jū, qù, xú, lǜ, nǚ.

On a separate note, if the tone is marked on the final i, the dot on the final i has to be expunged. Examples in this case: mī, bì, cí.

The neutral tone (or called the fifth tone) is unmarked in Mandarin Chinese language. Examples in this case: de, huan, xie, ma, bai.

When a syllable beginning with a, o or e follows another syllable, the syllable-dividing mark (') is used to avoid confusion. Examples: jiē versus jī'è ; fānàn versus fān'àn.

shù

Definition：perpendicular, vertical; erect

竖

竖 竖 竖 竖 竖 竖 竖
竖 竖 竖 竖 竖 竖 竖

立 R 9 Str

R: Radical

jùn

Definition：high, steep, towering; stern

峻

峻 峻 峻 峻 峻 峻 峻
峻 峻 峻 峻 峻 峻 峻

山 R 10 Str

R: Radical

lāo

Definition：scoop out of water; dredge, fish

捞

捞 捞 捞 捞 捞 捞 捞
捞 捞 捞 捞 捞 捞 捞

扌 R 10 Str

R: Radical

bǐ	Definition： mean; low
鄙	鄙 鄙 鄙 鄙 鄙 鄙 鄙 鄙 鄙 鄙 鄙 鄙 鄙 鄙
阝 R 13 Str R: Radical	

pò	Definition： vigor; body; dark part of moon
魄	魄 魄 魄 魄 魄 魄 魄 魄 魄 魄 魄 魄 魄 魄
鬼 R 14 Str R: Radical	

dōu	Definition： pouch
兜	兜 兜 兜 兜 兜 兜 兜 兜 兜 兜 兜 兜 兜 兜
儿 R 11 Str R: Radical	

hōng

Definition: coax; beguile, cheat, deceive

哄

哄 哄 哄 哄 哄 哄 哄
哄 哄 哄 哄 哄 哄 哄

口 R 9 Str

R: Radical

yǐng

Definition: rice tassel; sharp point; clever

颖

颖 颖 颖 颖 颖 颖 颖
颖 颖 颖 颖 颖 颖 颖

页 R 13 Str

R: Radical

xiè

Definition: bits, scraps, crumbs, fragments

屑

屑 屑 屑 屑 屑 屑 屑
屑 屑 屑 屑 屑 屑 屑

尸 R 10 Str

R: Radical

yǐ
Definition: ants
蚁
虫 R 9 Str
R: Radical
shèn
Definition: soak through, infiltrate
渗
氵 R 11 Str
R: Radical
tū
Definition: bald
秃
禾 R 7 Str
R: Radical

hàn	Definition： drought; dry; dry land
旱	旱 旱 旱 旱 旱 旱 旱
日 R 7 Str	
R: Radical	

qiǎn	Definition： reprimand, scold, abuse
谴	谴 谴 谴 谴 谴 谴 谴
	谴 谴 谴 谴 谴 谴 谴
讠 R 15 Str	谴 谴 谴 谴 谴 谴 谴
R: Radical	

dào	Definition： rice growing in field, rice plant
稻	稻 稻 稻 稻 稻 稻 稻
	稻 稻 稻 稻 稻 稻 稻
禾 R 15 Str	稻 稻 稻 稻 稻 稻 稻
R: Radical	

zhù

Definition： melt, cast; coin, mint

铸

钅 R 12 Str

R: Radical

huǎng

Definition： seemingly; absent-minded

恍

忄 R 9 Str

R: Radical

biǎn

Definition： decrease, lower; censure, criticize

贬

贝 R 8 Str

R: Radical

zhú

Definition： candle, taper; shine, illuminate

烛

火 R 10 Str

R: Radical

烛 烛 烛 烛 烛 烛 烛
烛 烛 烛 烛 烛 烛 烛

xiǔ

Definition： decayed, rotten; rot, decay

朽

木 R 6 Str

R: Radical

朽 朽 朽 朽 朽 朽 朽

yōng

Definition： commission fee

佣

亻 R 7 Str

R: Radical

佣 佣 佣 佣 佣 佣 佣

lù	Definition： rough, uneven, rocky; mediocre
碌	碌 碌 碌 碌 碌 碌 碌 碌 碌 碌 碌 碌 碌 碌
石 R 13 Str R: Radical	

qì	Definition： extend, reach; until; till
迄	迄 迄 迄 迄 迄 迄 迄
辶 R 6 Str R: Radical	

shēn	Definition： girdle; tie, bind; gentry
绅	绅 绅 绅 绅 绅 绅 绅 绅 绅 绅 绅 绅 绅 绅
纟 R 8 Str R: Radical	

bǎng	Definition： placard; list of successful exam candidates
榜	榜 榜 榜 榜 榜 榜 榜 榜 榜 榜 榜 榜 榜 榜
木 R 14 Str R: Radical	

sòng	Definition： recite, chant, repeat
诵	诵 诵 诵 诵 诵 诵 诵 诵 诵 诵 诵 诵 诵 诵
讠 R 9 Str R: Radical	

qín	Definition： birds, fowl; surname;; capture
禽	禽 禽 禽 禽 禽 禽 禽 禽 禽 禽 禽 禽 禽 禽
禸 R 12 Str R: Radical	

miáo	Definition： take aim at; look at
瞄	瞄 瞄 瞄 瞄 瞄 瞄 瞄 瞄 瞄 瞄 瞄 瞄 瞄 瞄
目 R 13 Str R: Radical	

chuáng	Definition： carriage curtain; sun screen
幢	幢 幢
巾 R 15 Str R: Radical	

dǔ	Definition： look at, gaze at; observe
睹	睹 睹 睹 睹 睹 睹 睹 睹 睹 睹 睹 睹 睹 睹
目 R 13 Str R: Radical	

huì	Definition: bribe; bribes; riches, wealth
贿	贿 贿 贿 贿 贿 贿 贿 贿 贿 贿 贿 贿 贿 贿
贝 R 10 Str R: Radical	

miè	Definition: disdain, disregard; slight
蔑	蔑 蔑 蔑 蔑 蔑 蔑 蔑 蔑 蔑 蔑 蔑 蔑 蔑 蔑
艹 R 14 Str R: Radical	

fù	Definition: to tie
缚	缚 缚 缚 缚 缚 缚 缚 缚 缚 缚 缚 缚 缚 缚
纟 R 13 Str R: Radical	

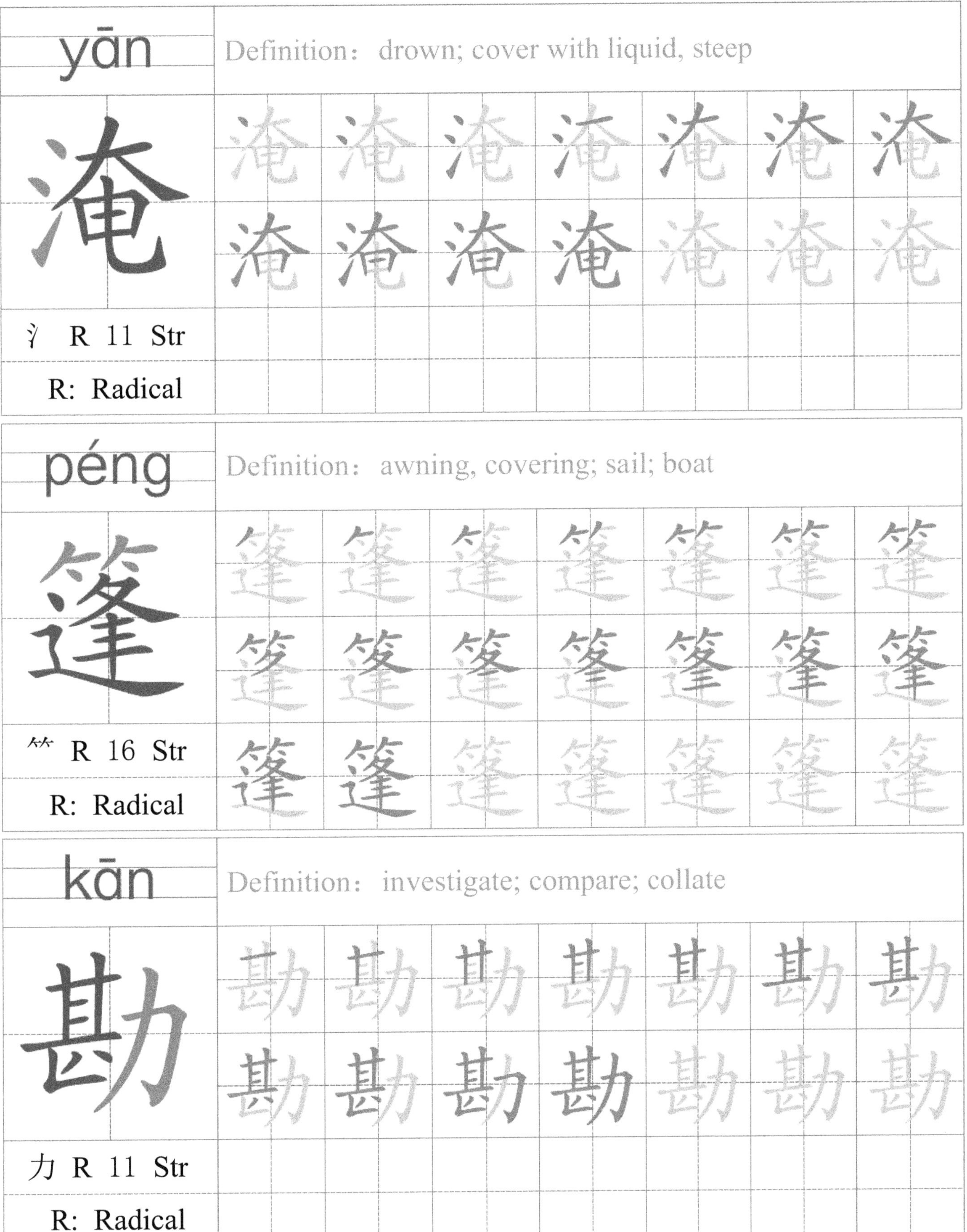

yān

Definition： drown; cover with liquid, steep

淹

氵 R 11 Str

R: Radical

péng

Definition： awning, covering; sail; boat

篷

⺮ R 16 Str

R: Radical

kān

Definition： investigate; compare; collate

勘

力 R 11 Str

R: Radical

càn

Definition： vivid, illuminating; bright

灿

火 R 7 Str

R: Radical

灿 灿 灿 灿 灿 灿 灿

chǎng

Definition： roomy, spacious, open, broad

敞

攵 R 12 Str

R: Radical

敞 敞 敞 敞 敞 敞 敞
敞 敞 敞 敞 敞 敞 敞

là

Definition： wax; candle; waxy, glazed; maggot; as a non-simplified form sometimes used as an equivalent to 禇,

蜡

虫 R 14 Str

R: Radical

蜡 蜡 蜡 蜡 蜡 蜡 蜡
蜡 蜡 蜡 蜡 蜡 蜡 蜡

gū

Definition: crime, criminal offense

辜

辛 R 12 Str

R: Radical

diàn

Definition: advance money, pay for another

垫

土 R 9 Str

R: Radical

dù

Definition: jealous, envious

妒

女 R 7 Str

R: Radical

yáo	Definition: sing; folksong, ballad; rumor
谣	谣 谣 谣 谣 谣 谣 谣 谣 谣 谣 谣 谣 谣 谣
讠 R 12 Str R: Radical	

zhěn	Definition: pillow
枕	枕 枕 枕 枕 枕 枕 枕 枕 枕 枕 枕 枕 枕 枕
木 R 8 Str R: Radical	

gài	Definition: beggar; beg; give
丐	丐 丐 丐 丐 丐 丐 丐
一 R 4 Str R: Radical	

mì

Definition： to seep out, excrete

泌

氵 R 8 Str

R: Radical

dīng

Definition： exhort or enjoin repeatedly

叮

口 R 5 Str

R: Radical

zhì

Definition： throw, hurl, cast, fling

擲

扌 R 11 Str

R: Radical

wǔ	Definition： insult, ridicule, disgrace
侮	侮 侮 侮 侮 侮 侮 侮 侮 侮 侮 侮 侮 侮 侮
亻 R 9 Str R: Radical	

shí	Definition： nibble away; erode; eclipse
蚀	蚀 蚀 蚀 蚀 蚀 蚀 蚀 蚀 蚀 蚀 蚀 蚀 蚀 蚀
虫 R 9 Str R: Radical	

shuāng	Definition： frost; crystallized; candied
霜	霜 霜
雨 R 17 Str R: Radical	

yùn	Definition： to collect, gather, store; profound
蕴	蕴 蕴
艹 R 15 Str R: Radical	

zhuāng	Definition： to adorn oneself, dress up, use make-up
妆	妆 妆 妆 妆 妆 妆 妆
女 R 6 Str R: Radical	

kǔn	Definition： tie up; bind, truss up; bundle
捆	捆 捆 捆 捆 捆 捆 捆 捆 捆 捆 捆 捆 捆 捆
扌 R 10 Str R: Radical	

bǐng	Definition：third; 3rd heavenly stem
丙	丙 丙 丙 丙 丙 丙 丙
一 R 5 Str R: Radical	

chāo	Definition：paper money, bank notes; copy
钞	钞 钞 钞 钞 钞 钞 钞 钞 钞 钞 钞 钞 钞 钞
钅 R 9 Str R: Radical	

quǎn	Definition：dog; radical number 94
犬	犬 犬 犬 犬 犬 犬 犬
犬 R 4 Str R: Radical	

gōng	Definition： body; personally, in person
躬	躬 躬 躬 躬 躬 躬 躬 躬 躬 躬 躬 躬 躬 躬
身 R 10 Str	
R: Radical	

zhòu	Definition： daytime, daylight
昼	昼 昼 昼 昼 昼 昼 昼 昼 昼 昼 昼 昼 昼 昼
日 R 9 Str	
R: Radical	

diàn	Definition： pay respect; settle
奠	奠 奠 奠 奠 奠 奠 奠 奠 奠 奠 奠 奠 奠 奠
大 R 12 Str	
R: Radical	

dǎo

Definition: stamp feet; dance

蹈

⻊ R 17 Str

R: Radical

蹈 蹈 蹈 蹈 蹈 蹈 蹈
蹈 蹈 蹈 蹈 蹈 蹈 蹈
蹈 蹈 蹈 蹈 蹈 蹈 蹈

lòu

Definition: narrow; crude, coarse; ugly

陋

阝 R 8 Str

R: Radical

陋 陋 陋 陋 陋 陋 陋
陋 陋 陋 陋 陋 陋 陋

lǚ

Definition: companion; associate with

侣

亻 R 8 Str

R: Radical

侣 侣 侣 侣 侣 侣 侣
侣 侣 侣 侣 侣 侣 侣

zhí	Definition： nephew
侄	侄 侄 侄 侄 侄 侄 侄 侄 侄 侄 侄 侄 侄 侄
亻 R 8 Str	
R: Radical	

nüè	Definition： cruel, harsh, oppressive
虐	虐 虐 虐 虐 虐 虐 虐 虐 虐 虐 虐 虐 虐 虐
虍 R 9 Str	
R: Radical	

duò	Definition： fall, sink, let fall; degenerate
堕	堕 堕 堕 堕 堕 堕 堕 堕 堕 堕 堕 堕 堕 堕
土 R 11 Str	
R: Radical	

jīng	Definition: stem, stalk
茎	茎 茎 茎 茎 茎 茎 茎 茎 茎 茎 茎 茎 茎 茎
艹 R 8 Str	
R: Radical	

lǎ	Definition: horn, bugle; lama; final particle
喇	喇 喇 喇 喇 喇 喇 喇 喇 喇 喇 喇 喇 喇 喇
口 R 12 Str	
R: Radical	

róng	Definition: silk, cotton, or woolen fabric
绒	绒 绒 绒 绒 绒 绒 绒 绒 绒 绒 绒 绒 绒 绒
纟 R 9 Str	
R: Radical	

jiǎo	Definition： disturb, agitate, stir up
搅	搅 搅 搅 搅 搅 搅 搅 搅 搅 搅 搅 搅 搅 搅
扌 R 12 Str R: Radical	

dì	Definition： tie, join, connect; connection
缔	缔 缔 缔 缔 缔 缔 缔 缔 缔 缔 缔 缔 缔 缔
纟 R 12 Str R: Radical	

jí	Definition： jealousy; be jealous of
嫉	嫉 嫉 嫉 嫉 嫉 嫉 嫉 嫉 嫉 嫉 嫉 嫉 嫉 嫉
女 R 13 Str R: Radical	

zào

Definition： kitchen stove, cooking stove

灶

灶 灶 灶 灶 灶 灶 灶

火 R 7 Str

R: Radical

gē

Definition： pigeon, dove; Columba species (various)

鸽

鸽 鸽 鸽 鸽 鸽 鸽 鸽

鸽 鸽 鸽 鸽 鸽 鸽 鸽

鸟 R 11 Str

R: Radical

wěi

Definition： woof; parallels of latitude

纬

纬 纬 纬 纬 纬 纬 纬

纟 R 7 Str

R: Radical

fèi

Definition: boil, bubble up, gush

沸

氵 R 8 Str

R: Radical

chóu

Definition: farmland, arable land; category

畴

田 R 12 Str

R: Radical

è

Definition: stop, suppress, curb, check; a bar

遏

辶 R 12 Str

R: Radical

shuò

Definition: shine, glitter, sparkle

烁

烁 烁 烁 烁 烁 烁 烁
烁 烁 烁 烁 烁 烁 烁

火 R 9 Str

R: Radical

xiù

Definition: smell, scent, sniff; olfactive

嗅

嗅 嗅 嗅 嗅 嗅 嗅 嗅
嗅 嗅 嗅 嗅 嗅 嗅 嗅

口 R 13 Str

R: Radical

bā

Definition: trumpet

叭

叭 叭 叭 叭 叭 叭 叭

口 R 5 Str

R: Radical

shē
Definition： extravagant, wasteful; exaggerate
奢
大 R 11 Str
R: Radical
zhuō
Definition： stupid, clumsy, crude; convention
拙
扌 R 8 Str
R: Radical
dòng
Definition： main beams supporting house
栋
木 R 9 Str
R: Radical

xiè

Definition： drain off, leak; flow, pour down

泻

氵 R 8 Str

R: Radical

泻 泻 泻 泻 泻 泻 泻
泻 泻 泻 泻 泻 泻 泻

wù

Definition： have interview with; meet

晤

日 R 11 Str

R: Radical

晤 晤 晤 晤 晤 晤 晤
晤 晤 晤 晤 晤 晤 晤

zhì

Definition： young, immature; childhood

稚

禾 R 13 Str

R: Radical

稚 稚 稚 稚 稚 稚 稚
稚 稚 稚 稚 稚 稚 稚

dǎo	Definition： hull; thresh; beat, attack
捣	捣 捣 捣 捣 捣 捣 捣 捣 捣 捣 捣 捣 捣 捣
扌 R 10 Str R: Radical	

gān	Definition： embarrassed; ill at ease
尴	尴 尴 尴 尴 尴 尴 尴 尴 尴 尴 尴 尴 尴 尴
尢 R 13 Str R: Radical	

gà	Definition： limp, staggering gait; embarrass
尬	尬 尬 尬 尬 尬 尬 尬
尢 R 7 Str R: Radical	

chà	Definition： be surprised, be shocked
诧	诧 诧 诧 诧 诧 诧 诧 诧 诧 诧 诧 诧 诧 诧
讠 R 8 Str R: Radical	

jué	Definition： prattle, be glib
噼	嚼 嚼
口 R 20 Str R: Radical	

kuàng	Definition： extensive, wide, broad; empty
旷	旷 旷 旷 旷 旷 旷 旷
日 R 7 Str R: Radical	

yá

Definition: bud, sprout, shoot

芽

芽 芽 芽 芽 芽 芽 芽

艹 R 7 Str

R: Radical

tàn

Definition: carbon

碳

碳 碳 碳 碳 碳 碳 碳

碳 碳 碳 碳 碳 碳 碳

石 R 14 Str

R: Radical

tì

Definition: be cautious, careful, alert

惕

惕 惕 惕 惕 惕 惕 惕

惕 惕 惕 惕 惕 惕 惕

忄 R 11 Str

R: Radical

xiōng	Definition： turbulent; noisy, restless
汹	汹 汹 汹 汹 汹 汹 汹
氵 R 7 Str R: Radical	

xīng	Definition： raw meat; rank, strong-smelling
腥	腥 腥 腥 腥 腥 腥 腥 腥 腥 腥 腥 腥 腥 腥
月 R 13 Str R: Radical	

chéng	Definition： purify water by allowing sediment to settle; clear, pure
澄	澄 澄
氵 R 15 Str R: Radical	

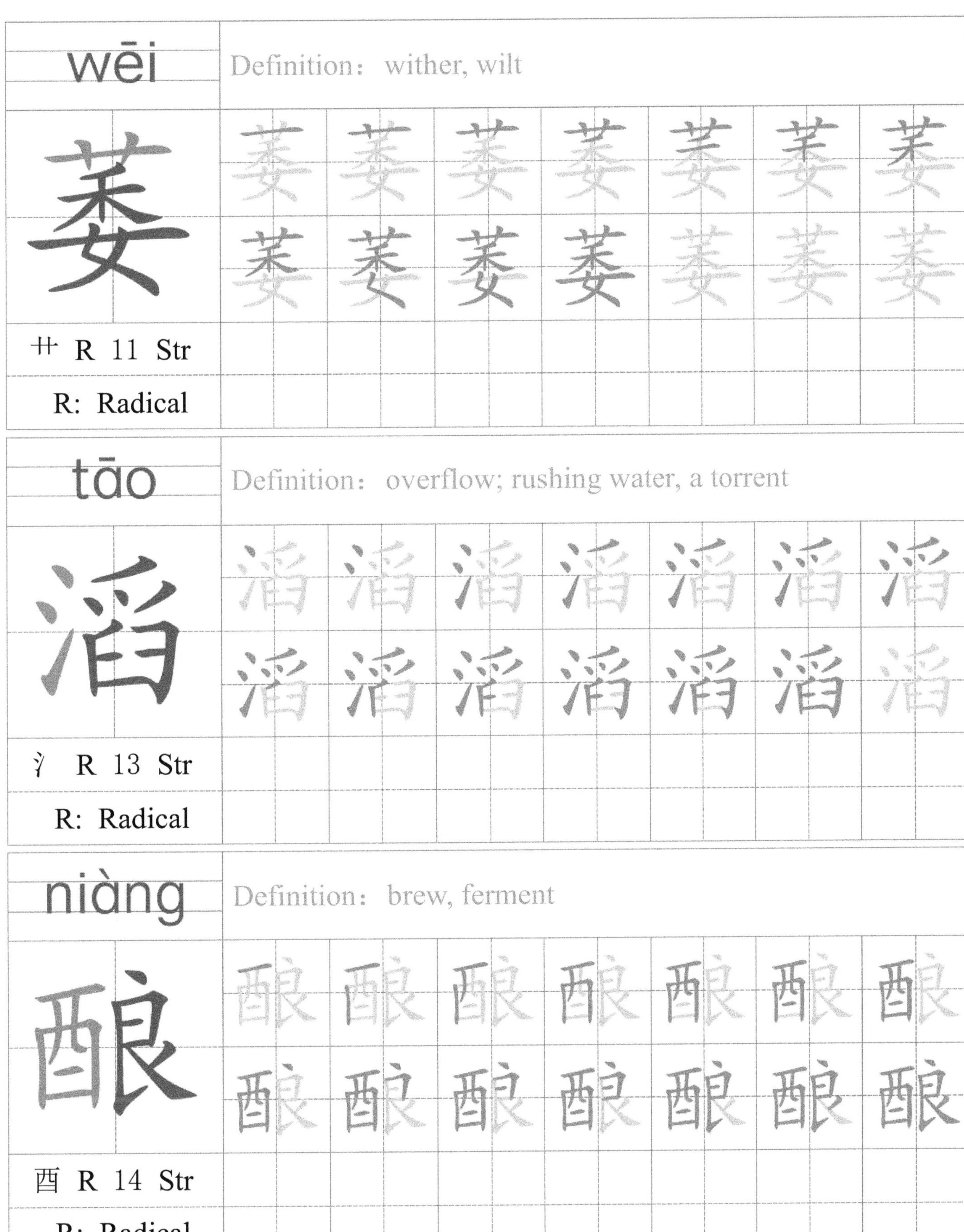
wēi
Definition： wither, wilt
萎
艹 R 11 Str
R: Radical
tāo
Definition： overflow; rushing water, a torrent
滔
氵 R 13 Str
R: Radical
niàng
Definition： brew, ferment
酿
酉 R 14 Str
R: Radical

jiè

Definition： warn, admonish; warning

诫

讠 R 9 Str

R: Radical

zōng

Definition： hemp palm; palm tree

棕

木 R 12 Str

R: Radical

xuān

Definition： lively, noisy; clamor, talk loudly

喧

口 R 12 Str

R: Radical

cì	Definition： serve, wait upon, attend; examine
伺	伺 伺 伺 伺 伺 伺 伺
亻 R 7 Str	
R: Radical	

shāo	Definition： pointed tip of something long like a branch; rudder
梢	梢 梢 梢 梢 梢 梢 梢 梢 梢 梢 梢 梢 梢 梢
木 R 11 Str	
R: Radical	

bà	Definition： embankment; dam
坝	坝 坝 坝 坝 坝 坝 坝
土 R 7 Str	
R: Radical	

fū	Definition： spread, diffuse; apply, paint
敷	敷 敷 敷 敷 敷 敷 敷
	敷 敷 敷 敷 敷 敷 敷
攵 R 15 Str R: Radical	敷 敷 敷 敷 敷 敷 敷

bì	Definition： cover, shield, shelter, protect
庇	庇 庇 庇 庇 庇 庇 庇
广 R 7 Str R: Radical	

náo	Definition： scratch; disturb, bother; submit
挠	挠 挠 挠 挠 挠 挠 挠
	挠 挠 挠 挠 挠 挠 挠
扌 R 9 Str R: Radical	

lǒu

Definition： hug, embrace; drag, pull

搂

扌 R 12 Str

R: Radical

zào

Definition： be noisy; chirp loudly

噪

口 R 16 Str

R: Radical

jià

Definition： sow grain; sheaves of grain

稼

禾 R 15 Str

R: Radical

qǐn	Definition： sleep, rest; bed chamber
寝	寝 寝 寝 寝 寝 寝 寝 寝 寝 寝 寝 寝 寝 寝
宀 R 13 Str	
R: Radical	

bǔ	Definition： chew food; feed
哺	哺 哺 哺 哺 哺 哺 哺 哺 哺 哺 哺 哺 哺 哺
口 R 10 Str	
R: Radical	

zhì	Definition： flag, pennant; sign; fasten
帜	帜 帜 帜 帜 帜 帜 帜 帜 帜 帜 帜 帜 帜 帜
巾 R 8 Str	
R: Radical	

róu

Definition： rub, massage; crush by hand

揉

扌 R 12 Str

R: Radical

nì

Definition： greasy, oily, dirty; smooth

腻

月 R 13 Str

R: Radical

tān

Definition： paralysis, palsy, numbness

瘫

疒 R 15 Str

R: Radical

mì	Definition： seek; search
觅	觅 觅 觅 觅 觅 觅 觅
	觅 觅 觅 觅 觅 觅 觅
见 R 8 Str	
R: Radical	

pì	Definition： out-of-the-way, remote; unorthodox
僻	僻 僻 僻 僻 僻 僻 僻
	僻 僻 僻 僻 僻 僻 僻
亻 R 15 Str	僻 僻 僻 僻 僻 僻 僻
R: Radical	

màn	Definition： creeping plants, tendrils, vines
蔓	蔓 蔓 蔓 蔓 蔓 蔓 蔓
	蔓 蔓 蔓 蔓 蔓 蔓 蔓
艹 R 14 Str	
R: Radical	

zǎ	Definition: question-forming particle, why? how? what?; to bite; loud
咋	咋 咋 咋 咋 咋 咋 咋 咋 咋 咋 咋 咋 咋 咋
口 R 8 Str	
R: Radical	

qiàn	Definition: inlay, set in; fall into; rugged
嵌	嵌 嵌 嵌 嵌 嵌 嵌 嵌 嵌 嵌 嵌 嵌 嵌 嵌 嵌
山 R 12 Str	
R: Radical	

pàn	Definition: boundary path dividing fields
畔	畔 畔 畔 畔 畔 畔 畔 畔 畔 畔 畔 畔 畔 畔
田 R 10 Str	
R: Radical	

sè

Definition： astringent; harsh; uneven, rough

涩

氵 R 10 Str

R: Radical

bèng

Definition： hop, leap, jump; bright

蹦

⻊ R 18 Str

R: Radical

dāo

Definition： talkative; quarrelous

叨

口 R 5 Str

R: Radical

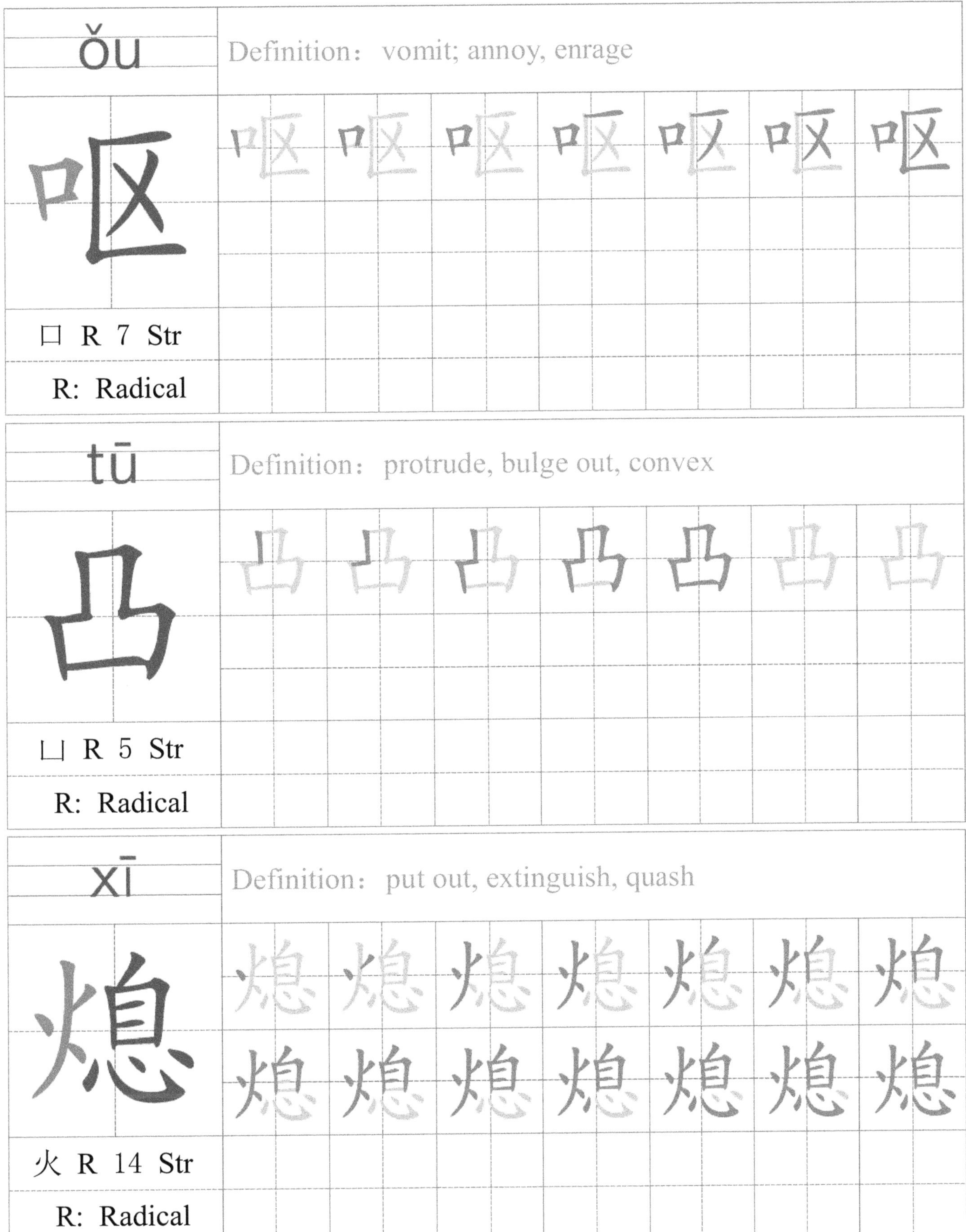
ǒu
Definition： vomit; annoy, enrage
呕
呕 呕 呕 呕 呕 呕 呕
口 R 7 Str
R: Radical
tū
Definition： protrude, bulge out, convex
凸
凸 凸 凸 凸 凸 凸 凸
凵 R 5 Str
R: Radical
xī
Definition： put out, extinguish, quash
熄
熄 熄 熄 熄 熄 熄 熄
熄 熄 熄 熄 熄 熄 熄
火 R 14 Str
R: Radical

shang	Definition： clothes; skirt; beautiful
裳	裳 裳 裳 裳 裳 裳 裳
	裳 裳 裳 裳 裳 裳 裳
衣 R 14 Str	
R: Radical	

āo	Definition： concave, hollow, depressed; a pass, valley
凹	凹 凹 凹 凹 凹 凹 凹
凵 R 5 Str	
R: Radical	

táng	Definition： chest; hollow space, cavity
膛	膛 膛 膛 膛 膛 膛 膛
	膛 膛 膛 膛 膛 膛 膛
月 R 15 Str	膛 膛 膛 膛 膛 膛 膛
R: Radical	

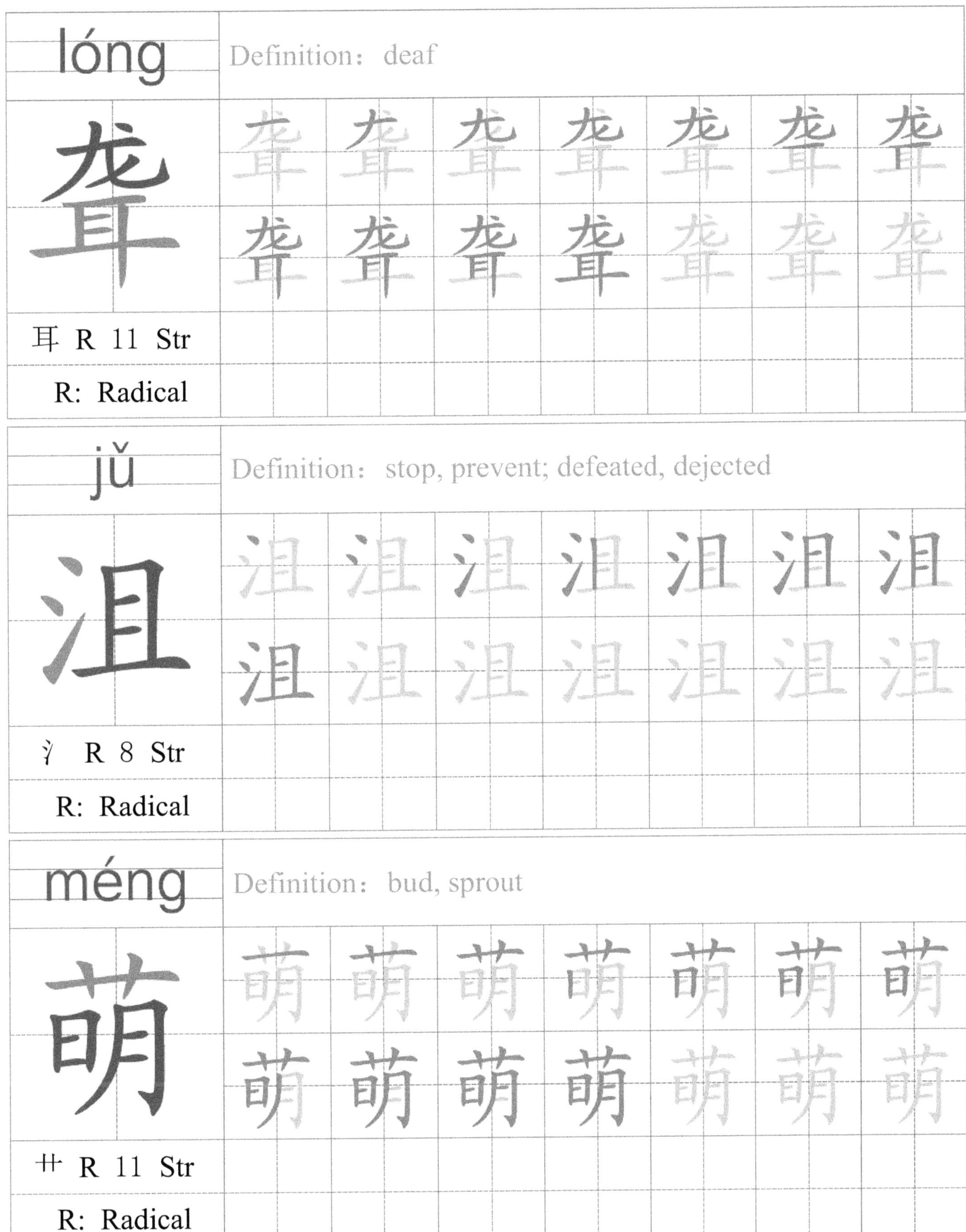
lóng
Definition： deaf
聋
耳 R 11 Str
R: Radical
jǔ
Definition： stop, prevent; defeated, dejected
沮
氵 R 8 Str
R: Radical
méng
Definition： bud, sprout
萌
艹 R 11 Str
R: Radical

piē	Definition： discard, abandon, throw away
撇	撇 撇 撇 撇 撇 撇 撇 撇 撇 撇 撇 撇 撇 撇
扌 R 14 Str	
R: Radical	

gǒu	Definition： careless, frivolous; illicit; grammatical particle: if, but, if only; surname; grass name; distinguish DKW
苟	苟 苟 苟 苟 苟 苟 苟 苟 苟 苟 苟 苟 苟 苟
艹 R 8 Str	
R: Radical	

mǎ	Definition： ant; leech
蚂	蚂 蚂 蚂 蚂 蚂 蚂 蚂 蚂 蚂 蚂 蚂 蚂 蚂 蚂
虫 R 9 Str	
R: Radical	

jiǎn
Definition： temperate, frugal, economical
俭
亻 R 9 Str
R: Radical
tiē
Definition： invitation card; notice
帖
巾 R 8 Str
R: Radical
jiān
Definition： fry in fat or oil; boil in water
煎
灬 R 13 Str
R: Radical

shù

Definition： villa, country house

墅

墅 墅 墅 墅 墅 墅 墅
墅 墅 墅 墅 墅 墅 墅

土 R 14 Str

R: Radical

líng

Definition： lonely, solitary; actor

伶

伶 伶 伶 伶 伶 伶 伶

亻 R 7 Str

R: Radical

dǎi

Definition： bad, vicious, depraved, wicked

歹

歹 歹 歹 歹 歹 歹 歹

歹 R 4 Str

R: Radical

kuò	Definition： broad, wide, open, empty; to expand
廓	廓 廓 廓 廓 廓 廓 廓 廓 廓 廓 廓 廓 廓 廓
广 R 13 Str R: Radical	

huì	Definition： conceal; shun; regard as taboo
讳	讳 讳 讳 讳 讳 讳 讳
讠 R 6 Str R: Radical	

bàn	Definition： petal; segment; valves
瓣	瓣 瓣
瓜 R 19 Str R: Radical	

wǎng

Definition： useless, in vain; bent, crooked

枉

枉 枉 枉 枉 枉 枉 枉
枉 枉 枉 枉 枉 枉 枉

木 R 8 Str

R: Radical

zuó

Definition： polish jade; cut jade

琢

琢 琢 琢 琢 琢 琢 琢
琢 琢 琢 琢 琢 琢 琢

王 R 12 Str

R: Radical

jī

Definition： ridicule, jeer, mock; inspect

讥

讥 讥 讥 讥 讥 讥 讥

讠 R 4 Str

R: Radical

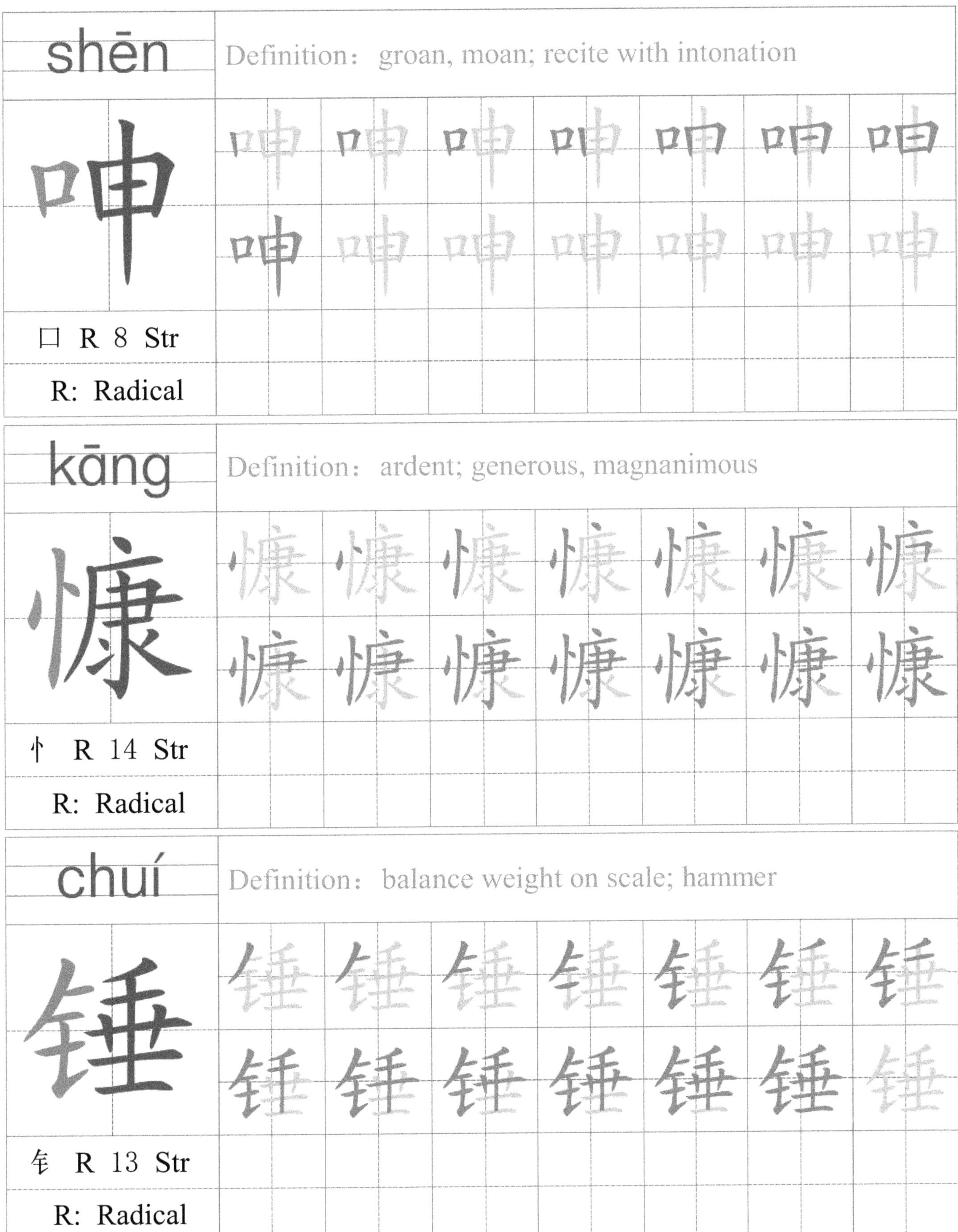
shēn
Definition： groan, moan; recite with intonation
呻
口 R 8 Str
R: Radical
kāng
Definition： ardent; generous, magnanimous
慷
忄 R 14 Str
R: Radical
chuí
Definition： balance weight on scale; hammer
锤
钅 R 13 Str
R: Radical

jiǎng	Definition： oar, paddle
桨	桨 桨 桨 桨 桨 桨 桨
	桨 桨 桨 桨 桨 桨 桨
木 R 10 Str	
R: Radical	

bàng	Definition： pound; weigh
磅	磅 磅 磅 磅 磅 磅 磅
	磅 磅 磅 磅 磅 磅 磅
石 R 15 Str	磅 磅 磅 磅 磅 磅 磅
R: Radical	

kuì	Definition： offer food superior; send gift
馈	馈 馈 馈 馈 馈 馈 馈
	馈 馈 馈 馈 馈 馈 馈
饣 R 12 Str	
R: Radical	

jiàn	Definition： sprinkle, spray; spill, splash
溅	溅 溅 溅 溅 溅 溅 溅 溅 溅 溅 溅 溅 溅 溅
氵 R 12 Str	
R: Radical	

gài	Definition： calcium
钙	钙 钙 钙 钙 钙 钙 钙 钙 钙 钙 钙 钙 钙 钙
钅 R 9 Str	
R: Radical	

zhāng	Definition： clear, manifest, obvious
彰	彰 彰 彰 彰 彰 彰 彰 彰 彰 彰 彰 彰 彰 彰
彡 R 14 Str	
R: Radical	

mī	Definition： be blinded
眯	眯 眯 眯 眯 眯 眯 眯 眯 眯 眯 眯 眯 眯 眯
目 R 11 Str	
R: Radical	

ABOUT THE AUTHOR

Jia Sheng Low is a Mandarin Chinese language teacher that served the community under the Malaysia's Ministry of Education. He graduated from the Institute of Teacher Education of Malaysia in 2011 with Honors in Postgraduate Advanced Professional Diploma in Education (Chinese Studies). He teaches Mandarin Chinese language for both native and non-native learners since 2009. Connect with Mr. Low at https://learnchinese-mandarin.blogspot.com.

Want to explore more Learn Chinese books?

Visit this URL now:

https://LearnChineseBooks.blogspot.com

www.ingramcontent.com/pod-product-compliance
Ingram Content Group UK Ltd.
Pitfield, Milton Keynes, MK11 3LW, UK
UKHW061829190726
13853UKWH00009B/2507